**Save the King!**
Single Letter Sounds A~M   6

 **The White Mountain**
Single Letter Sounds N~Z   16

 **The Sea Palace**
Short Vowel a/e/i   26

 **The Volcano's Dragon**
Short Vowel o/u   36

 **The Pirate Cave**
Long Vowel a/i   46

 **In the Maze**
Long Vowel o/u — 56

 **At the North Pole**
Double Letter Sounds — 66

At the Witch's Castle
Double Letter Sounds — 76

 **In the Big Trouble**
Double Letter Sounds — 86

 **The King is Alive!**
Double Letter Sounds — 96

Introduction

This book is composed of 10 interesting stories.

Phonics Story

Students can review phonics skills learned in phonics book 1~5 and practice reading a fun, easy story composed of target words.

Phonics Review

Phonics Review provides exercises for the students to practice the sounds they learned.
The exercises help students to expand their word skills and recognize the sounds.

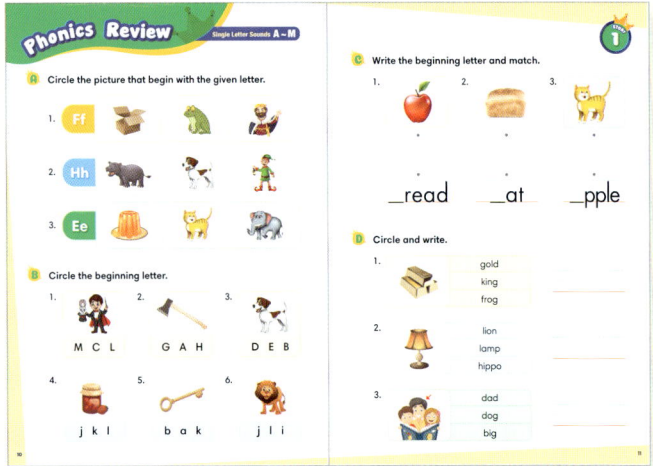

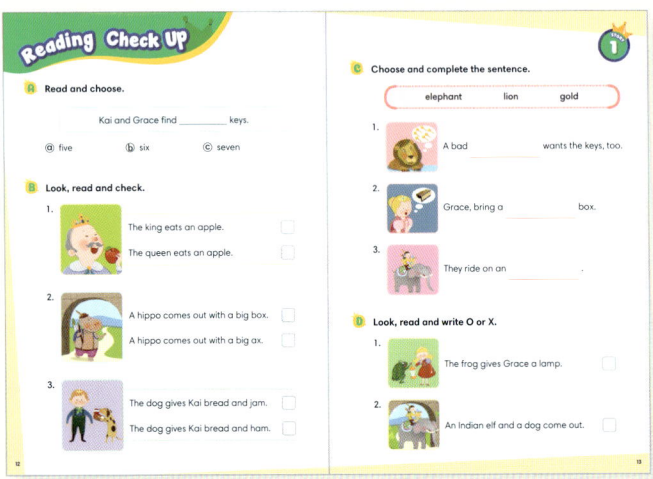

Reading Check Up

Reading Check Up provides exercises for the students to practice the stories they learned.
The exercises help students better understand the stories.

Fun Time

Students can practice the target words through the various activities and games. Have fun with various activities!

Let's Chant

Students can practice the reading stories through the chants. Sing along with the chants!

Digital Book for Teachers (PC)

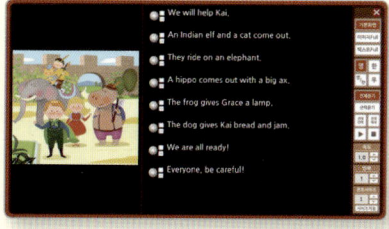

Online Study for Students (PC & Mobile App)

STORY 1: Save the King!

Track 1-2

One day, the king eats an apple.

But he sleeps.

It is a bad apple.

 "Dad! Dad!"

 "Grace, bring a gold box."

KEYWORDS

king	apple	bad	dad	gold	box

The magic jelly can awake the king.

It is in the box.

 "Kai, find seven keys.

The keys can open this box."

A bad lion wants the keys, too.

 magic     jelly    key    lion

 "We will help Kai."

An Indian elf and a cat come out.

They ride on an elephant.

A hippo comes out with a big ax.

KEYWORDS

| Indian | elf |  cat | elephant |  hippo | 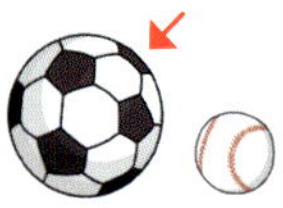 big |  ax |

The frog gives Grace a lamp.

The dog gives Kai bread and jam.

 "We are all ready!"

 "Everyone, be careful!"

 frog

 lamp

 dog

 bread

 jam

Phonics Review

Single Letter Sounds A ~ M

 A Circle the picture that begin with the given letter.

1. Ff

2. Hh

3. Ee

B Circle the beginning letter.

1.
M C L

2.
G A H

3.
D E B

4.
j k l

5.
b a k

6.
j l i

C Write the beginning letter and match.

1.    2.    3.

_read   _at   _pple

D Circle and write.

1.    gold / king / frog   _____

2.    lion / lamp / hippo   _____

3.    dad / dog / big   _____

Reading Check Up

A Read and choose.

Kai and Grace find _____ keys.

ⓐ five　　　　ⓑ six　　　　ⓒ seven

B Look, read and check.

1. The king eats an apple. ☐
   The queen eats an apple. ☐

2. A hippo comes out with a big box. ☐
   A hippo comes out with a big ax. ☐

3. The dog gives Kai bread and jam. ☐
   The dog gives Kai bread and ham. ☐

 Choose and complete the sentence.

| elephant   lion   gold |

1. A bad _____ wants the keys, too.

2. Grace, bring a _____ box.

3. They ride on an _____ .

D Look, read and write O or X.

1. The frog gives Grace a lamp. ☐

2. An Indian elf and a dog come out. ☐

Fun Time

Help Kai and Grace find the keys.

Let's Chant!

One day, the king eats an apple.
But it is a bad apple.

The magic jelly can awake the king.
Kai and Grace find seven keys.

An Indian elf and a cat come out.
A hippo comes out with a big ax.

The frog gives Grace a lamp.
The dog gives Kai bread and jam.

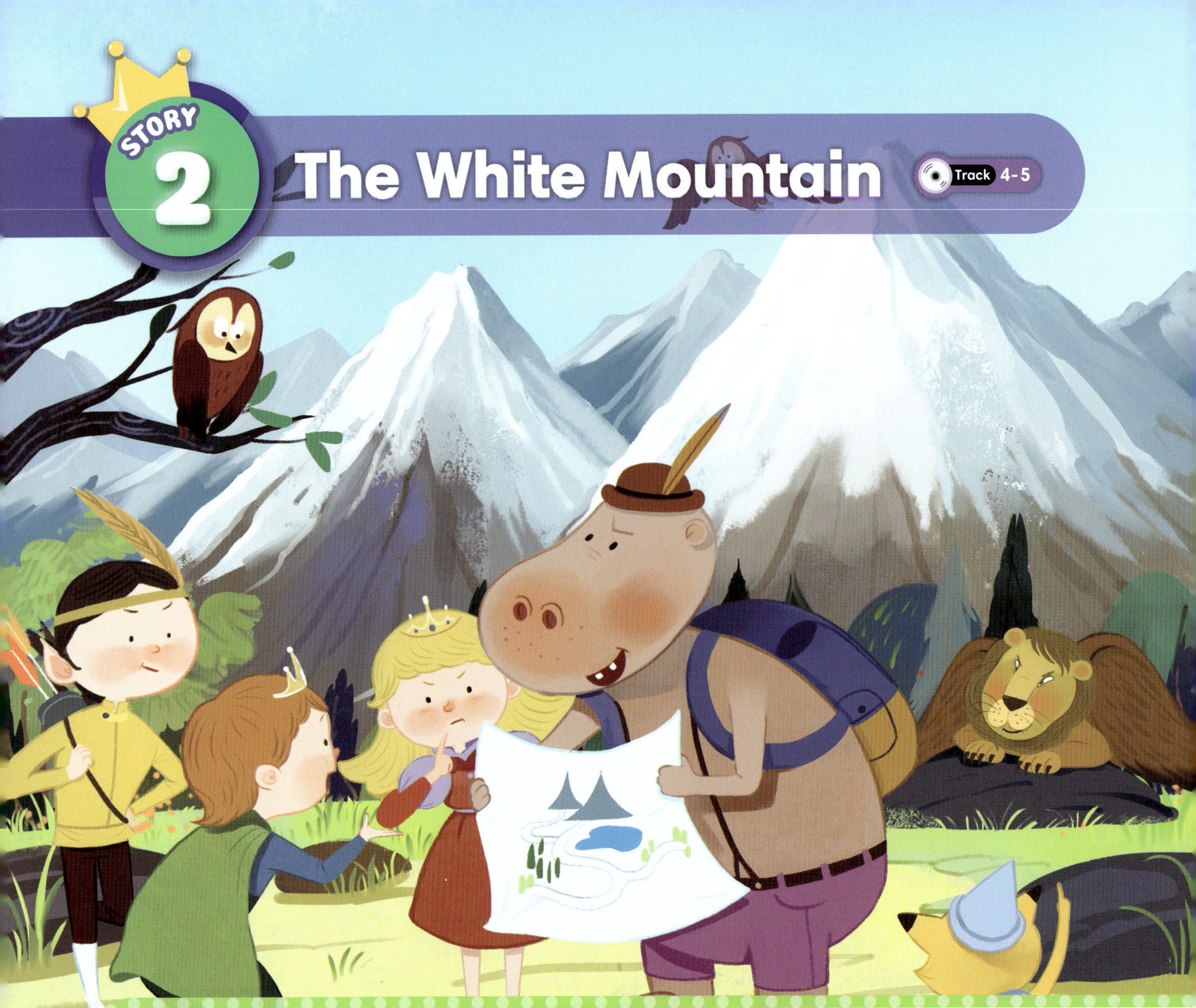

STORY 2: The White Mountain

"Look at the White Mountain!"

"The owl is in the sky."

"I have a question. How can we go to the top?"

"We have a map."

"He he! I have wings. I can fly."

KEYWORDS

 white

 owl

 sky

 question

 top

 wing

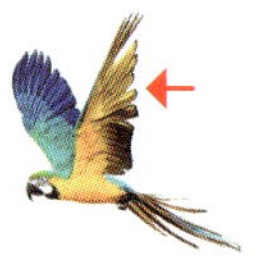

 "Yak knows about the key."

The lion catches Yak with a net.

 "Where is the key?"

 "I cannot tell you."

 "I have no time. Go on!"

 "Uh! Help me!"

 yak

 net

 time

 "Are you okay? We can help you."

 "Thank you."

 "Where is the key?"

 "The key is in a red tent.

　　The tent is on the top."

KEYWORDS

red

tent

 "Oh, no! We slip!"

 "Don't worry. Zebra, Ox and Panda! Make a ladder."

 "Let's go up!"

 "Yay! We find the first key."

 "Oh, no! I am too late."

zebra

ox

panda

up

Phonics Review

Single Letter Sounds N~Z

A. Match and say the word.

1. **p**
2. **w**
3. **z**

__anda   __hite   __ebra

B. Circle the beginning letter.

1.
   v t n x

2.
   m r w x

3.
   u t s q

4.
   z r y u

5.
   o u p v

6.
   t n m y

20

C Unscramble and write the word.

1.

2.

3.

4.

 D Change the first letter and write.

1. **ax**

   Change the **a** to **o**.

2. **bed**

   Change the **b** to **r**.

3. **ring**

   Change the **r** to **w**.

21

Reading Check Up

 A Read and choose.

> The first key is _____.

ⓐ on the top of the White Mountain
ⓑ on the top of the Black Mountain
ⓒ over the White Mountain

 B Read and choose the correct answer.

1. What is in the sky?

| owl | ox | yak |

2. What does the lion have?

| map | wings | ladder |

3. Where is the key?

| white tent | red tent | yellow tent |

 Choose, write and number.

> top　　　　White　　　　net

1. Look at the _____ Mountain!

2. The lion catches Yak with a _____.

3. The tent is on the _____.

 Read, look and number.

> 1. I have a question. How can we go to the top?
> 2. Zebra, Ox and Panda! Make a ladder.

Fun Time

Write the correct word in the box.

| tent | sky | ox | top |
| panda | yak | zebra | net |

Let's Chant!

Look at the White Mountain!
How can we go up the top?

Yak knows about the key.
The lion catches Yak with a net.

Are you okay? We can help you.
The key is in a red tent.

Zebra, Ox and Panda! Make a ladder.
Yay! We find the first key.

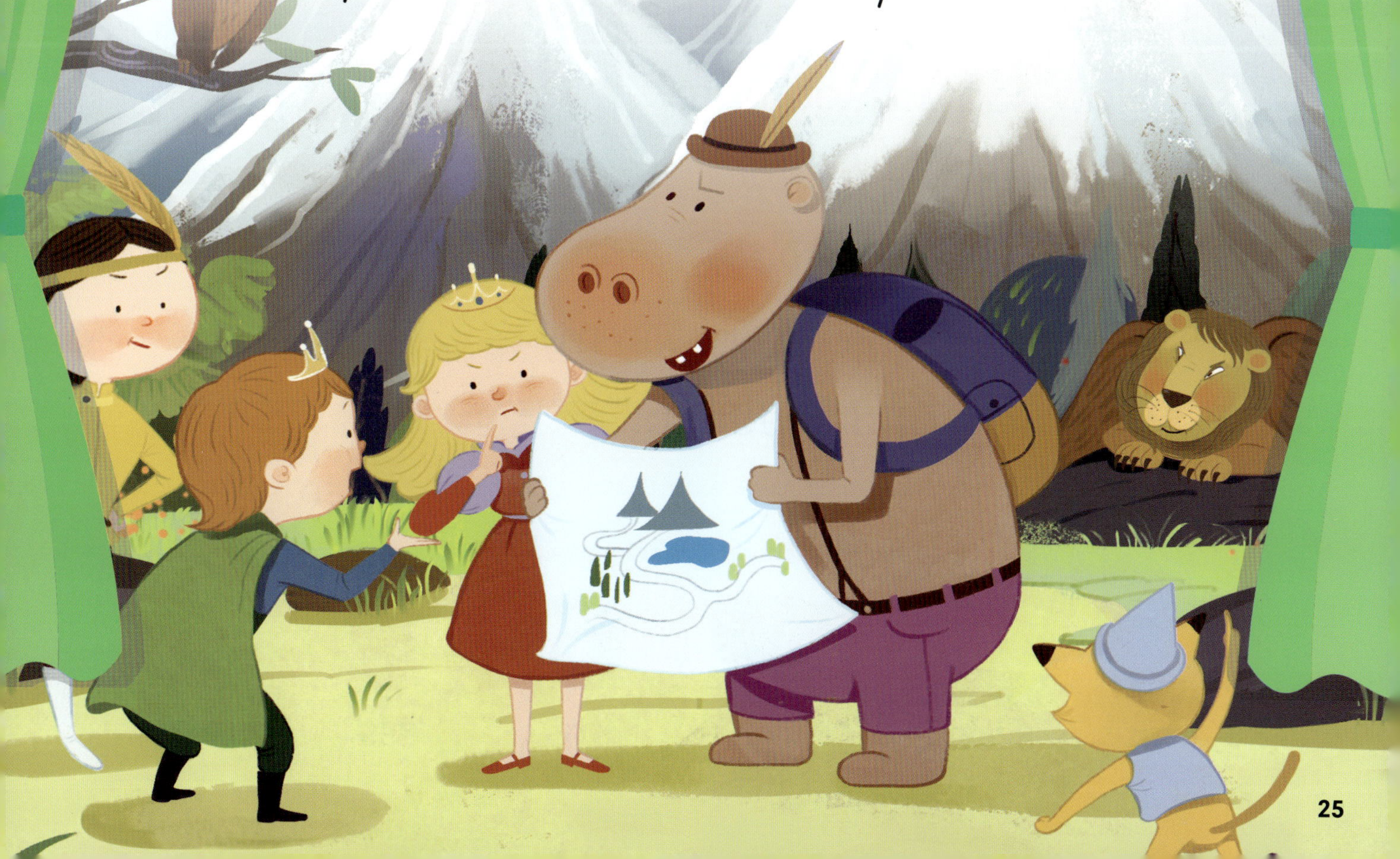

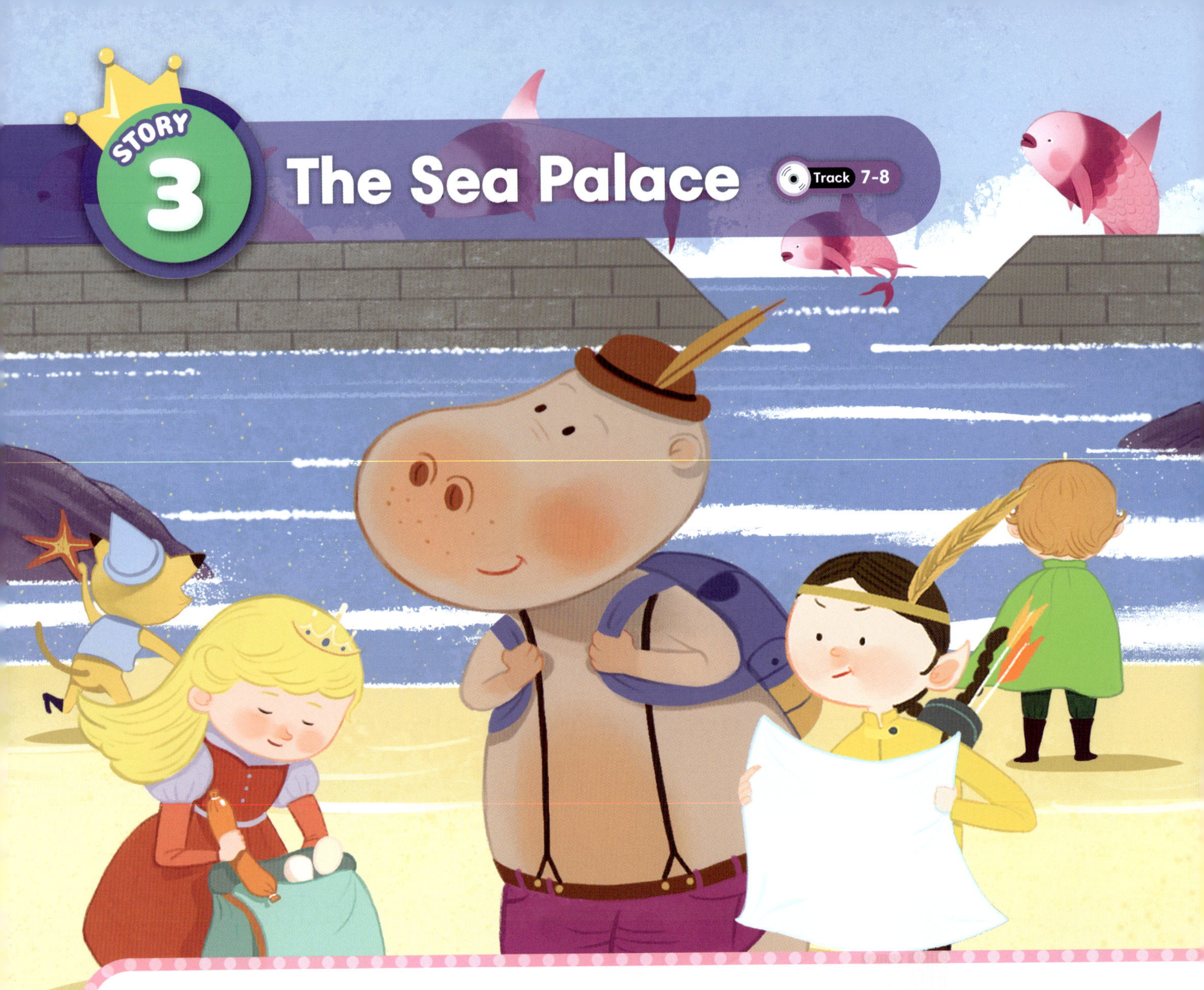

STORY 3: The Sea Palace

"The second key is in the sea palace.

How can we get there?"

"We have the map.

The sea is over the dam."

"Ham and six eggs are in my bag.

Eat them and cheer up!"

KEYWORDS

 map

 dam

 ham

 six

 egg

 bag

The lion looks at the Mermaid Princess.

He puts on a red wig.

He catches the Mermaid Princess with a net.

 "Dad! Help me!"

 "Give me the key."

 "You are a mad man!"

red	 wig	net	dad	mad	man

"You look sad."

"The bad lion takes my princess."

"We can help you. Everyone, hold on to the fish's fin."

"The lion sleeps on the bed.
Cat, hit the lion's leg."

KEYWORDS

							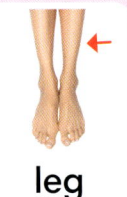
sad	bad	fish	fin	bed	cat	hit	leg

 "Hurry up! Take the Mermaid Princess."

 "No. Stop there!"

 "Thank you.

You are the best. Here is the key."

 "Wow! We find the second key."

best

Phonics Review

Short Vowel a / e / i

A Circle the correct piece.

1.  m — ap / an / am

2.  c — ag / at / ad

3. 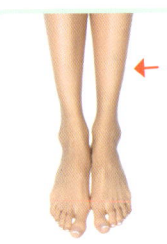 l — et / ed / eg

4.  f — it / in / ig

B Circle the word with the same vowel sound.

1.  dad / bed

2.  six / mad

3.  red / wig

4.  hit / sad

C Circle the word and write.

e g g b e s t s i x w i g s a d d a m m a p

1.

2.

3.

D Circle and write.

1.

| bad |
| bed |
| dad |

2.

| hit |
| cat |
| net |

3.

| leg |
| wig |
| bag |

Reading Check Up

 A Read and choose.

> The bad lion takes _____.

ⓐ the king of the sea
ⓑ the Mermaid Princess
ⓒ the Mermaid Prince

 B Look, read and choose.

1.

   You look _____.

   ⓐ mad
   ⓑ sad
   ⓒ dad

2.

   The lion sleeps on the _____.

   ⓐ net
   ⓑ dam
   ⓒ bed

3.

   _____ are in my bag.

   ⓐ Bread and jam
   ⓑ Ham and six eggs
   ⓒ Maps

 C Read and circle T or F.

1. The sea is over the dam.　　T　F
2. The lion puts on a red wig.　　T　F
3. The cat hits the lion's head.　　T　F

D Look, read and number in order.

The lion sleeps on the bed.

He catches the Mermaid Princess with a net.

Everyone, hold on to the fish's fin.

You are the best.

Fun Time

🌏 **Look, write and say the word.**

1.  rhymes with

   dam

2.  rhymes with

   dad

3.  rhymes with

   cap

4.  rhymes with

   red

5.  rhymes with

   big

34

Let's Chant!

The second key is in the sea palace.
Ham and six eggs are in my bag.

The lion puts on a red wig.
He catches the Mermaid Princess with a net.

Everyone, hold on to the fish's fin.
The lion sleeps on the bed.

Cat, hit the lion's leg.
You are the best. Here is the key.

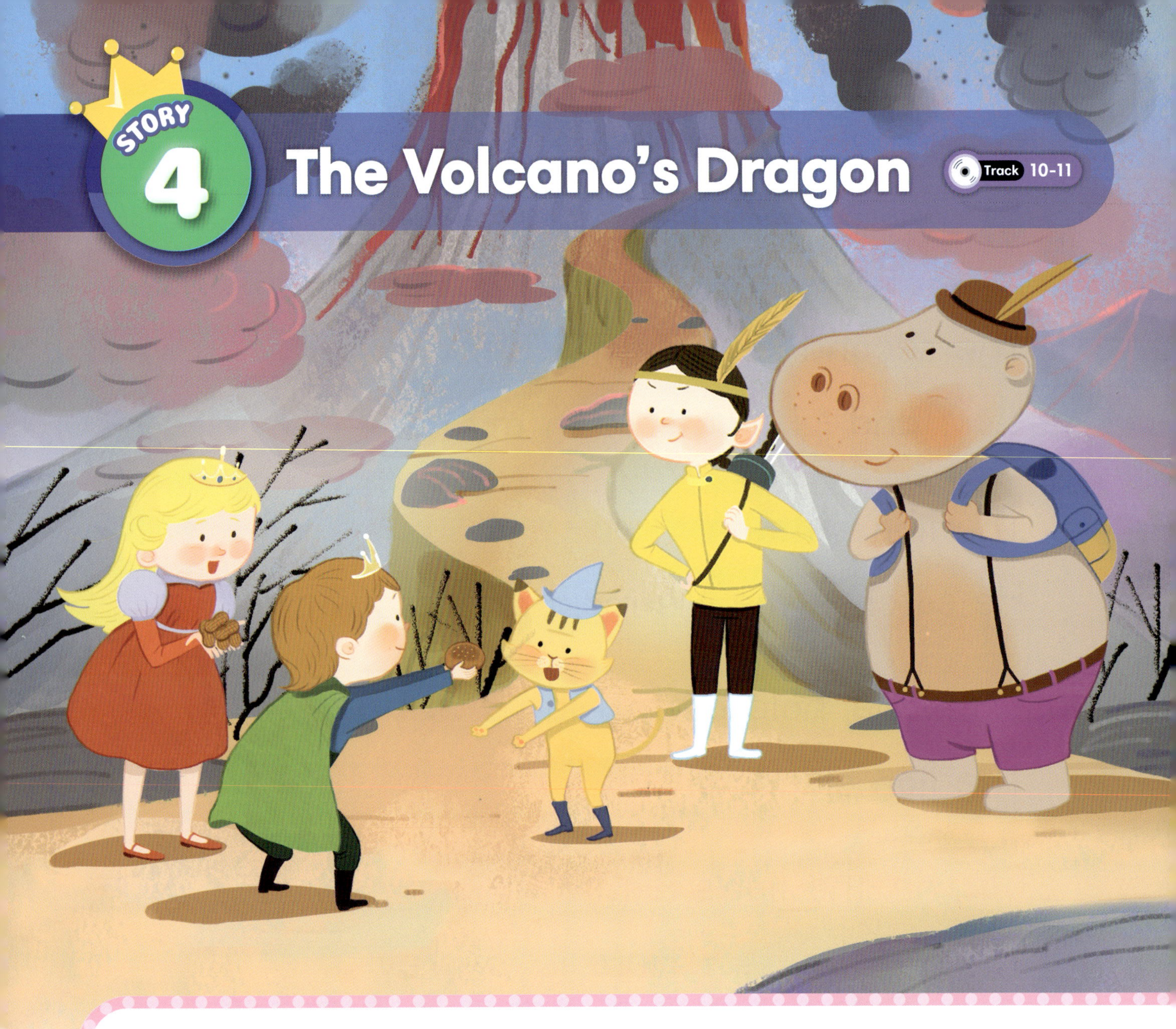

STORY 4 The Volcano's Dragon

Track 10-11

There is a volcano.

It is hot and there are fogs.

 "Kai and Grace stay here."

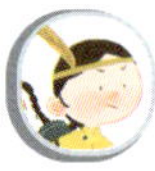

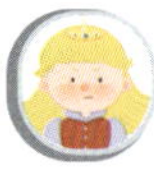

 "Here are nuts and bun."

 "Everyone, be careful."

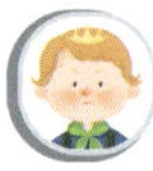

KEYWORDS

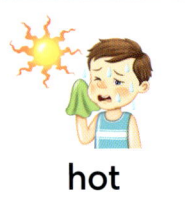

hot

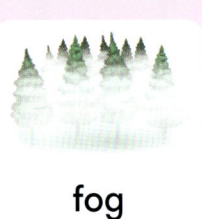

fog

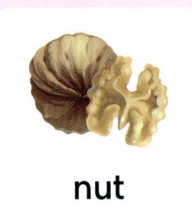

nut

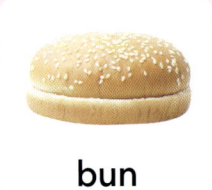

bun

 "The key is on the top.

There are a fox and her cubs.

Let's go up with me."

 "No! I cannot leave my cubs here."

 "Be quiet! We will run."

top

fox

cub

run

 "Help! I am locked in this hut."

A big rock is next to the hut.

They jump over the rock and open the door.

 "Thank you. Here, ride on this rug."

KEYWORDS

lock	hut	rock	jump	rug

 "Wow! I got here first! Give me the key."

 "Who wakes me up? Hoo."

 "That's hot! Let's run away."

 "Hippo, give the dragon this gum."

 "OK, OK! Here is the key."

up

gum

Phonics Review

Short Vowel o / u

A Circle the correct piece.

1. h — ot / og / op

2. r — ut / ub / ug

3. r — ox / ock / ump

4. b — ut / un / um

B Circle the pictures with the same vowel sound.

1. top

2. hut

C Complete the crossword puzzle and number.

1.
2. f f x
      g

3.
   r
4. c   b
   n

D Change the first letter and write.

1. **run**

   Change the **r** to **b**.

2. **hut**

   Change the **h** to **n**.

3. **rock**

   Change the **r** to **l**.

Reading Check Up

A Read and choose.

_____ has the third key.

ⓐ Goddess of fire
ⓑ The volcano's dragon
ⓒ A fox

B Look, read and check.

1. A big lock is next to the nut. ☐
   A big rock is next to the hut. ☐

2. It is hot and there are fogs. ☐
   It is hot and there are rugs. ☐

3. Hippo, give the dragon this gum. ☐
   Hippo, give the dragon this bun. ☐

 Choose and complete the sentence.

| jump | cubs | nuts |

1. Here are _____ and bun.

2. There are a fox and her _____.

3. They _____ over the rock.

 Look, read and write O or X.

1. I am locked in this hut. ☐

2. Here, ride on this rug. ☐

Fun Time

Match, complete and write the word.

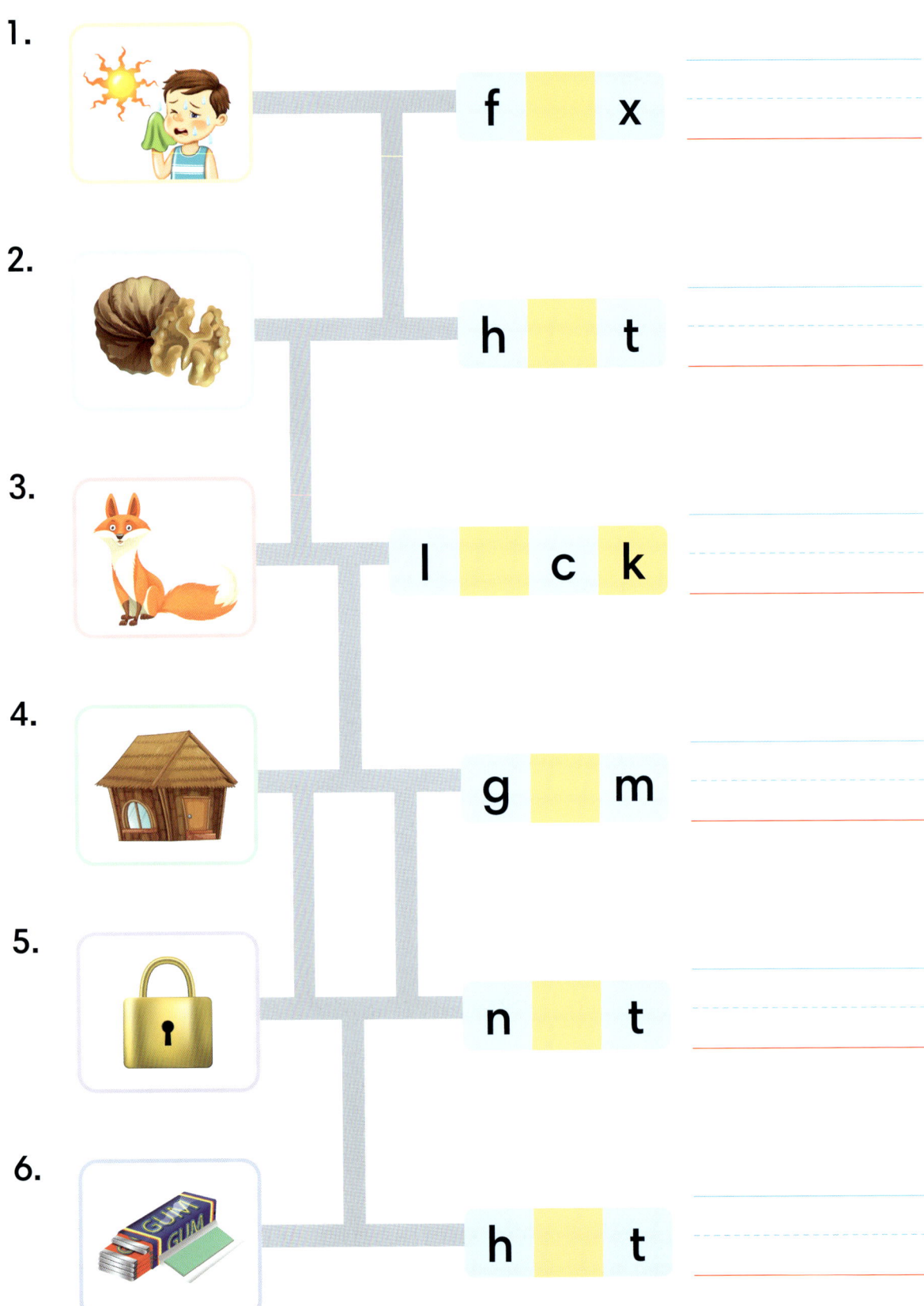

1. fox
2. hut
3. lock
4. gum
5. nut
6. hut

Let's Chant!

Track 12

The volcano is hot and there are fogs.
The key is on the top of the volcano.

Help! I am locked in this hut.
A big rock is next to the hut.

They jump over the rock and open the door.
Thank you. Here, ride on this rug.

Who wakes me up? Hoo.
Hippo, give the dragon this gum.

STORY 5: The Pirate Cave

Track 13-14

"The fourth key is in the Pirate Cave. I hate the pirates. They are very greedy."

"Where is the Pirate Cave?"

"Look at the kite with a pirate mark. There are many waves."

KEYWORDS

 cave

 hate

 kite

 wave

 "Captain, let's change your key with my jewels."
 "OK! I like jewels!"
 "Wait, Captain! They are just stones."
 "No, no. Where is the gate?"

The lion runs away.

like

wait

gate

The lion takes the mice.

 "We can win the game."

 "Captain, the lion brings mice."

Nine ships come in a line.

Mice shoot tires at the Pirate Cave.

Boom! Boom!

KEYWORDS

 take

 mice

 game

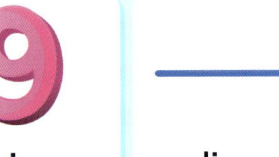 nine line

 tire

 "Let's help the pirates."

 "Fire! Fire!"

 "Dive into the water!"

 "Thank you. Here is the key. We will now be good men."

fire

dive

Phonics Review

Long Vowel a / i

A Circle the rhyming word.

1.  wait / wave

2.  line / like

3.  kite / hate

4.  tire / take

B Check the picture with the same vowel sound.

1. cave

2. mice

3. take

4. like
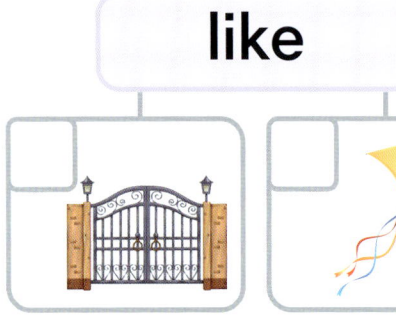

C. Complete the word and match.

1.
2.
3.

h_t_   l_k_   m_c_

D. Circle and write.

1.
   - cave
   - wave
   - dive

2.
   - take
   - gate
   - game

3.
   - fire
   - tire
   - kite

Reading Check Up

A Read and choose.

> The lion brings _____.

ⓐ pirates　　　ⓑ mice　　　ⓒ jewels

B Look, read and check.

1.
   - I like jewels! ☐
   - I hate jewels! ☐

2.
   - Mice shoot tires at the Pirate Cave. ☐
   - Mice shoot fires at the Pirate Cave. ☐

3.
   - Line ships come in a nine. ☐
   - Nine ships come in a line. ☐

C Choose, write and number.

| waves   kite   hate |

1. I _____ the pirates.

2. Look at the _____ with a pirate mark.

3. There are many _____.

D Read, look and number.

1. No, no. Where is the gate?
2. Dive into the water!

Fun Time

🦆 **Write and circle the picture.**

♥ = w   ♠ = n   ♣ = t   ♦ = g

♥ ave

♠ ine

♦ ate

♣ ire

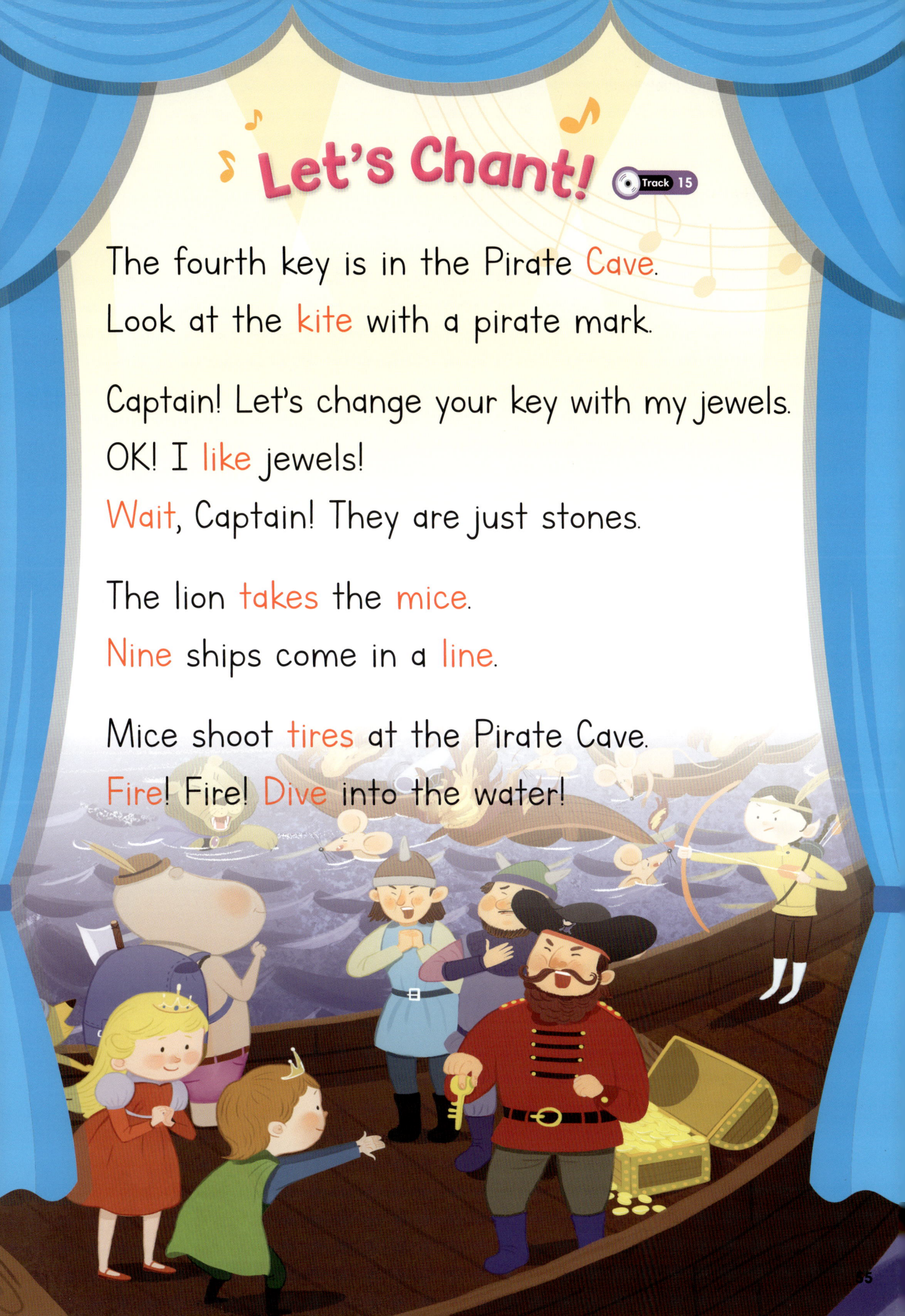

Let's Chant!

Track 15

The fourth key is in the Pirate Cave.
Look at the kite with a pirate mark.

Captain! Let's change your key with my jewels.
OK! I like jewels!
Wait, Captain! They are just stones.

The lion takes the mice.
Nine ships come in a line.

Mice shoot tires at the Pirate Cave.
Fire! Fire! Dive into the water!

STORY 6: In the Maze

Track 16-17

 "Row the boat.

The key is in the Bat's Blue Castle.

The bat's cave is under the dune."

 "Wow! This is a huge maze."

 "Use the rope."

KEYWORDS

row	boat	blue	dune	huge	use	rope

 "I ride the mule.

Oh! This is the bat's cave.

I will break this maze with fuse.

The key is mine. That is my hope. BAM!"

 "Oh, no! Our home is in danger."

mule

fuse

hope

home

"Oh, no! The cave falls! Let's run away.

Ouch! My bones break.

Oh~ I can't move."

"The Bat's Castle is in danger.

Let's help them!"

KEYWORDS

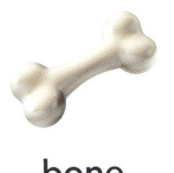
bone

move

 "Put the dome back.
Glue the broken parts."

 "Thank you so much.
Take this fruit and juice.
The key is in this cube."

dome

glue

fruit

juice

cube

Phonics Review

Long Vowel o / u

A Circle the correct piece.

1. r — ope / one / ow
2. d — uge / une / use
3. b — one / ope / oat
4. c — ove / ube / lue

B Check the picture with the same vowel sound.

1. hope
2. use
3. home
4. fruit

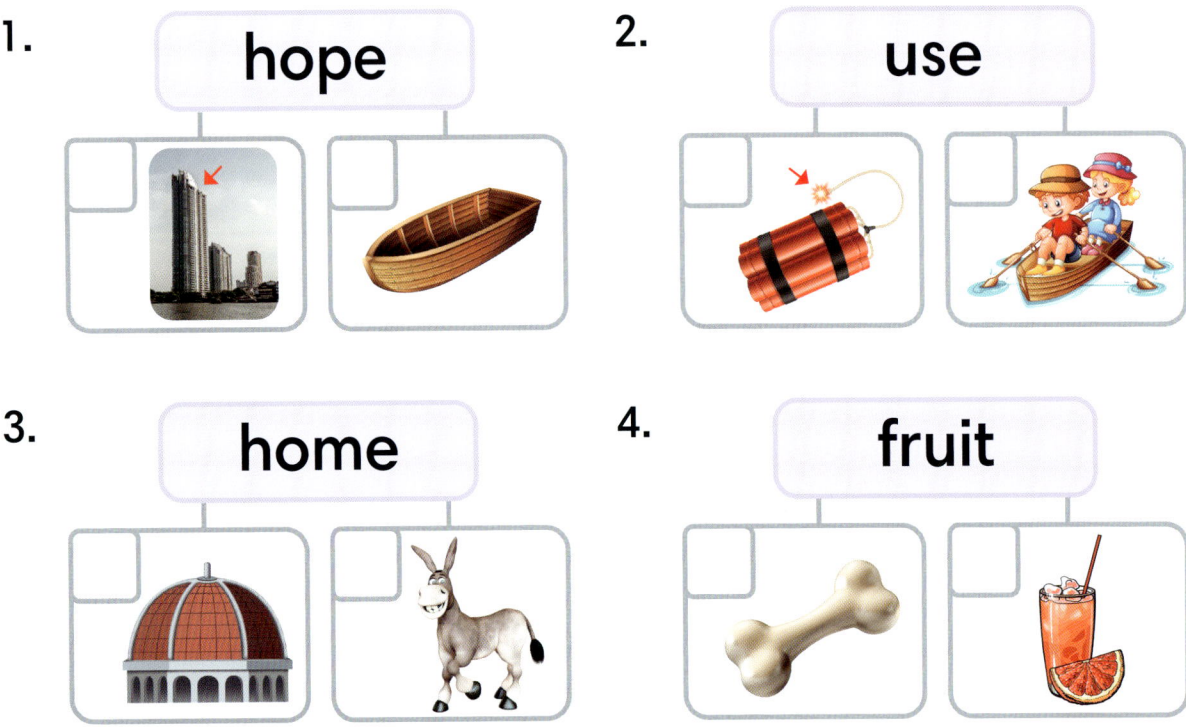

C Choose and complete the word.

-oat   -uge   -lue

1.  b____
2.  b____
3.  h____

D Change the first letter and write.

1. **cow**
   Change the **c** to **r**.

2. **home**
   Change the **h** to **d**.

3. **blue**
   Change the **b** to **g**.

Reading Check Up

 A Read and choose.

> The bat's cave is _____ the dune.

ⓐ on
ⓑ under
ⓒ over

 B Look, read and choose.

1.

    This is a _____ maze.

    ⓐ use
    ⓑ huge
    ⓒ fuse

2.

    Use the _____.

    ⓐ row
    ⓑ rope
    ⓒ hope

3.

    _____ the broken parts.

    ⓐ Clue
    ⓑ Blue
    ⓒ Glue

C. Read and circle T or F.

1. The key is in the Bat's Green Castle.   T   F

2. The Bat's Castle is in danger.   T   F

3. The key is in the cube.   T   F

D. Look, read and number in order.

Ouch! My bones break.

Put the dome back.

I ride the mule.

I will break this maze with fuse.

Fun Time

Look and follow the words.

Let's Chant!

Row the boat.
The key is in the Bat's Blue Castle.

I will break this maze with fuse.
Oh, no! Our home is in danger.
Ouch! My bones break. Oh~ I can't move.

Put the dome back.
Glue the broken parts.
Take this fruit and juice.

The key is in this cube.

STORY 7: At the North Pole

Track 19-20

"Today, I will choose my son-in-law."

"Paul! You must win!

Take this plate of fruit and bread."

"Mmm.. It smells good! I check the blade on my sled."

"I will shake the green flag."

KEYWORDS

 plate
 fruit
 bread
 smell
 blade
 sled
 green
 flag

"Nice! I will win and get the key.

Hurry up and go! This is smoke!"

"I can't see!

My sled breaks."

smoke

break

 "Let's help Paul."

 "Give a new sled to him."

 "Thank you. Let's go!"

 "Throw the bad lion in jail.

And close the door. Crab, keep him!"

KEYWORDS

close

crab

"Clap for Paul. Blow the trumpet and hit the drum! My princess, put on a pretty dress. Brush your hair. You are a beautiful bride."

"This key is for you."

"Thank you! Congratulations!"

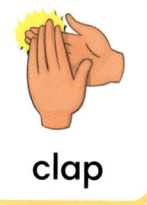						
clap	blow	trumpet	drum	dress	brush	bride

Phonics Review

Double Letter Sounds

 A Choose and write the numbers.

dr

bl

sm

1.
2.
3.
4.
5.
6.

B Check the picture that begin with the given letters.

1. **fl**
2. **cr**
3. **br**
4. **cl**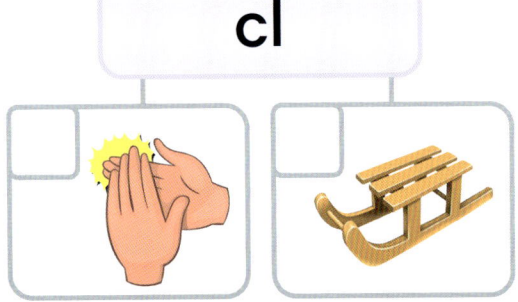

C Circle and complete the word.

1.

   fr   br

2.

   gr   dr

3.

   fr   cr

___ide   ___een   ___uit

D Circle and complete the sentence.

1.

   Take this _____ of fruit and bread.

   plate / blade

2.

   _____ your hair.

   Bread / Brush

71

Reading Check Up

 A Read and choose.

_____ is a beautiful bride.

ⓐ The polar bear king
ⓑ The polar bear Paul
ⓒ The polar bear princess

 B Read and choose the correct answer.

1. What will the polar bear princess shake?

gray flag   green flag   white flag

2. Who keeps the bad lion?

Hippo   Crab   Paul

3. What does the polar bear princess put on?

skirt   blouse   dress

C. Choose and complete the sentence.

> blow   blade   clap

1. I check the _____ on my sled.

2. _____ for Paul.

3. _____ the trumpet!

D. Look, read and write O or X.

1. It smells bad!

2. I can't see! My sled breaks.

Fun Time

Complete the puzzles.

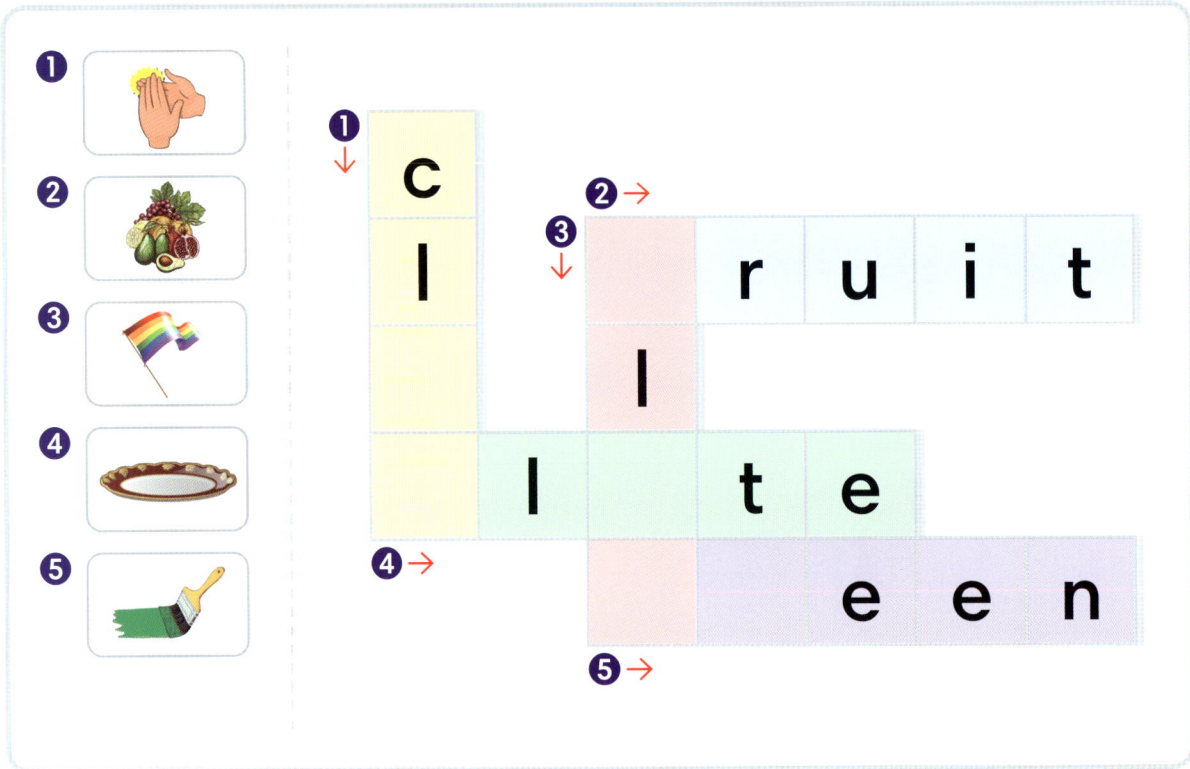

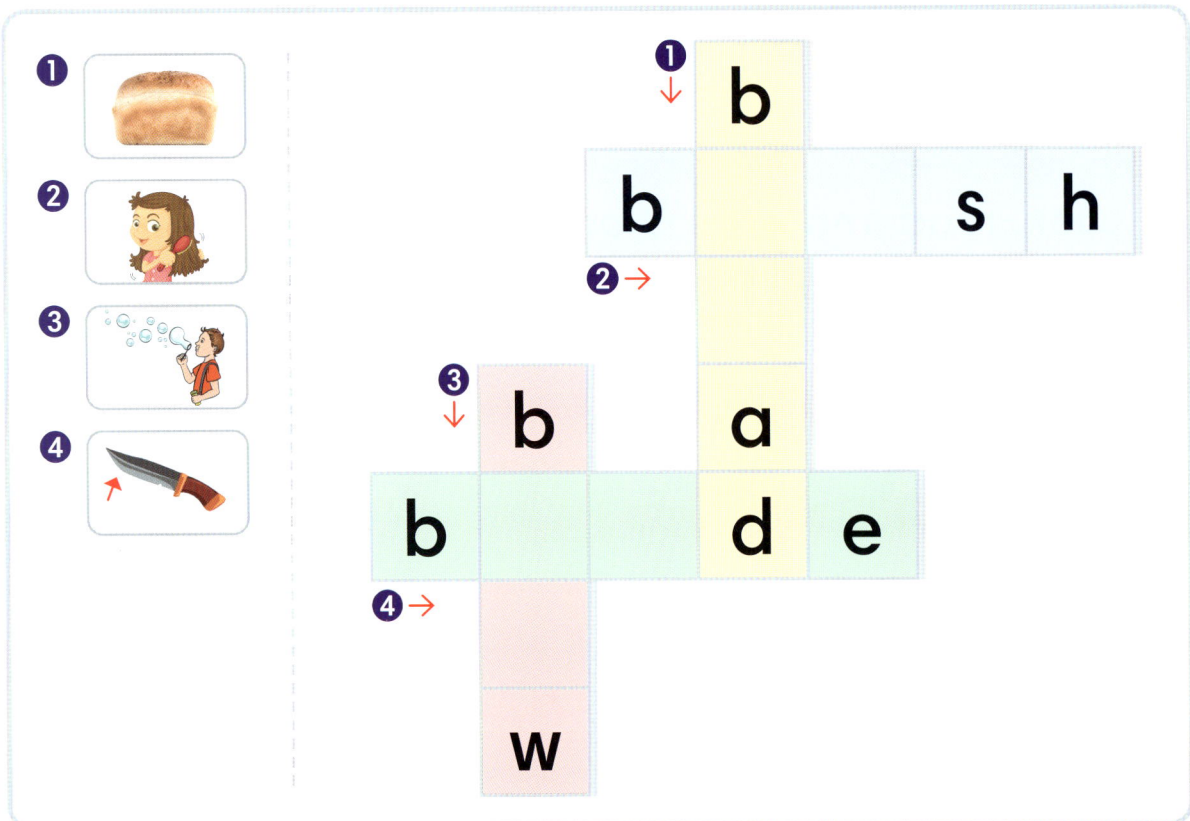

Let's Chant!

Take this plate of fruit and bread.

I will shake the green flag.

This is smoke! I can't see!

My sled breaks.

Give a new sled to Paul.

Throw the bad lion in jail. And close the door.

Clap for Paul. Blow the trumpet and hit the drum!

My Grace, put on a pretty dress.

You are a beautiful bride.

STORY 8 — At the Witch's Castle

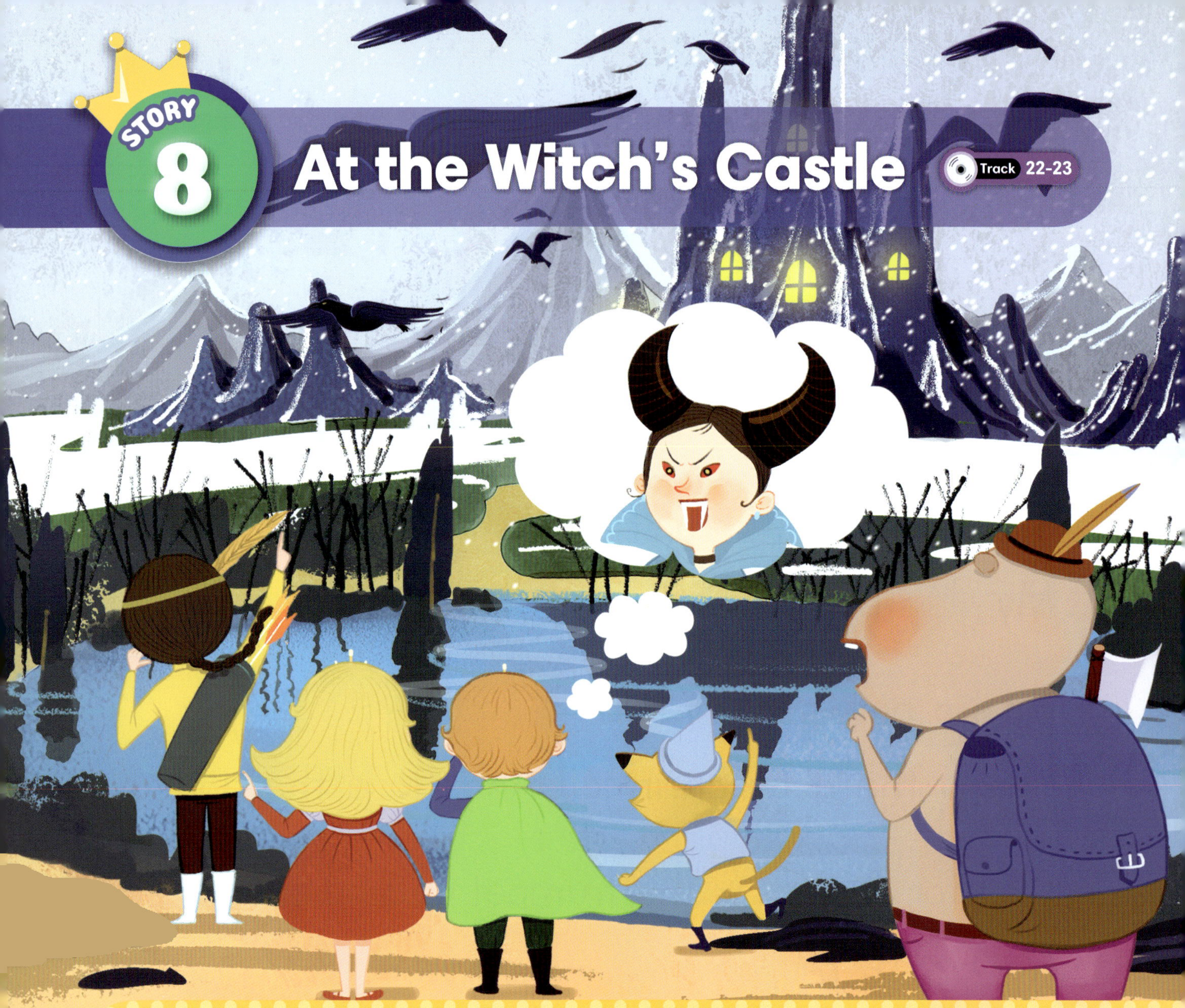

 "Look at the Witch's Castle!"

 "There is too much snow.

There is no spring.

The witch has sharp teeth. I am scared."

KEYWORDS

				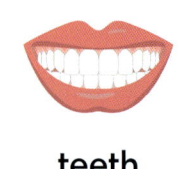
witch	snow	spring	sharp	teeth

 "Hi, Witch! Long time no see.

You have many spiders and snakes."

 "Yes. Eat this sweet cherry."

 "Thank you. Your skin looks young."

 "I eat a white duck every day.

And I drink white wine."

spider	 snake	sweet	cherry	skin	young	 white	duck	drink

 "Let's play a game.

Who can change into a sheep first? Go!

Wow! Now a small ant!"

 "It is easy."

 "Ha ha. I got you! Give me the key!"

KEYWORDS

sheep

ant

 "Let's help the witch."

 "Skunk! Fart on the bad lion!"

 "Oh, stop! Help me!"

 "Thank you for helping me. Take this key."

skunk

stop

Phonics Review

Double Letter Sounds

 A Match and say.

1. sk
2. sp
3. sn

 B Check the picture that have the given letters.

1. st
2. sw
3. ch
4. sh

C Circle, complete the words and match.

1.

   ch   wh

2.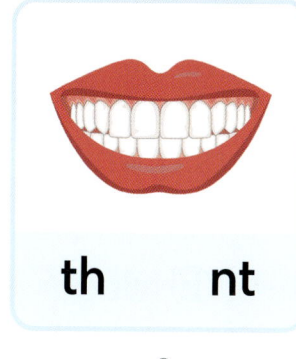

   th   nt

3.

   nk   ck

du___   tee___   wit___

D Unscramble and complete the sentence.

1.

   There is no _____.

   g n i p r s

2.

   Now a small _____.

   t a n

Reading Check Up

A Read and choose.

> The witch eats a white _____ every day.

ⓐ sheep   ⓑ duck   ⓒ ant

B Look, read and check.

1. There is too much smoke. ☐
   There is too much snow. ☐

2. Your skin looks young. ☐
   Your skunk looks young. ☐

3. Eat this sweet cherry. ☐
   Eat this sweet wine. ☐

C **Choose, write and number.**

> spiders   teeth   wine

1. The witch has sharp _____.

2. You have many _____ and snakes.

3. I drink white _____.

  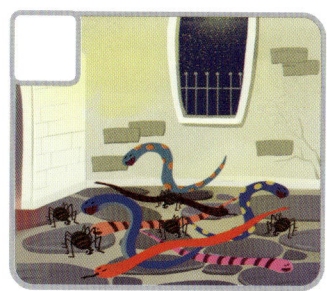

D **Read, look and number.**

1. Who can change into a sheep first? Go!
2. Skunk! Fart on the bad lion!

Fun Time

Look at the picture and find the word.

1.
2.
3.
4.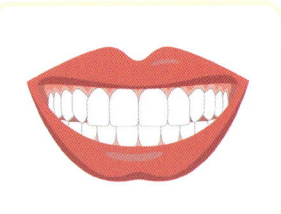
5.
6.

c	s	t	s	p	a	a	r
s	p	s	p	r	i	n	g
t	i	u	i	y	t	t	n
d	u	c	d	u	c	k	k
t	e	t	e	e	t	h	h
c	h	e	r	r	y	r	y

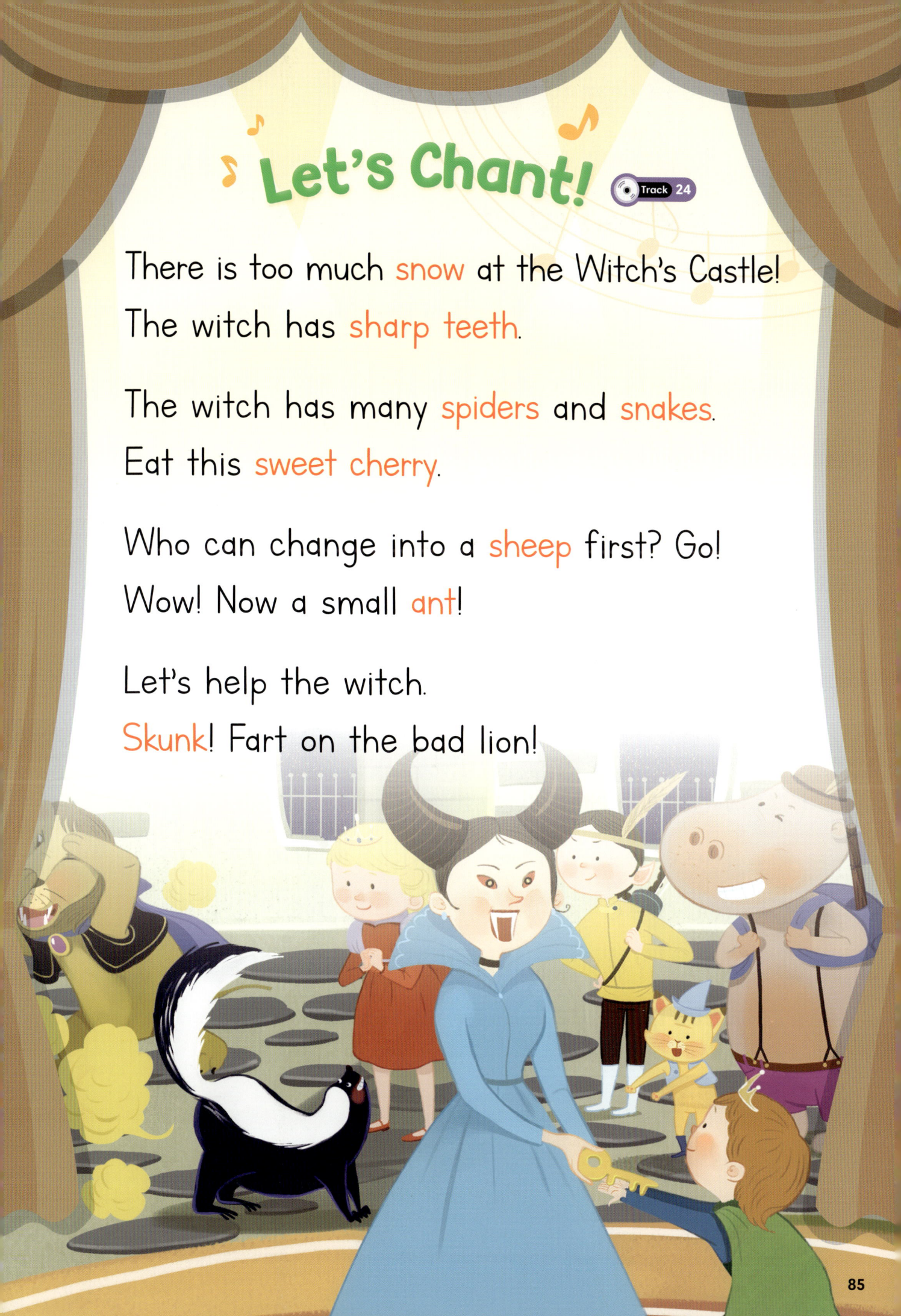

STORY 9 — In the Big Trouble

Track 25-26

"Wow! We found all the seven keys!
The queen will be very happy. This is a great joy."

"You are a boy but you are brave."

"The sky is gray. It is going to rain or snow.
Let's hurry up."

KEYWORDS

 key

 joy

 boy

 gray

 rain

 snow

 "Everyone, please help us.

My mom is very sick."

 "What? Let's go and help her.

Oh, no! That is a bad lion."

 "Good job. I will pay you with coins.

Chain them up."

coin

chain

 "Wow! All seven keys are mine!

I will be the king!

Now, how can I kill them?

Oh, good idea! I will push them off to the sea.

I am hungry. I want toast and tea.

KEYWORDS

sea

toast

tea

 "We lost all our keys."

 "Boo hoo. What should I do?"

 "Let's find a way."

 "The coil blocks the window."

 "Let's pray to God. Oh, Deer! Please mail a message to our friends."

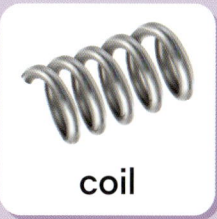
coil

window

pray

deer

mail

Phonics Review

Double Letter Sounds

 Choose and write the words.

-oy

-ai-

-ea

1.
2.
3.
4.
5.
6.

B **Check the picture that have the given letters.**

1. **ay**
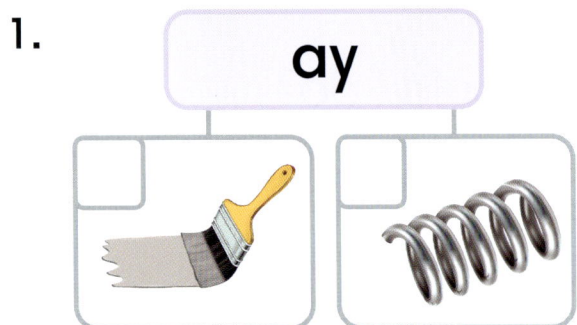

2. **oi**

3. **ey**

4. **ow**
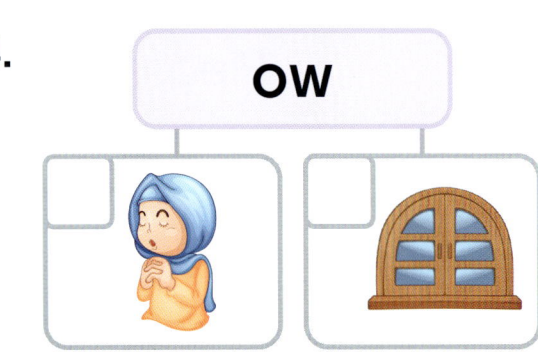

 Unscramble, write and match.

1.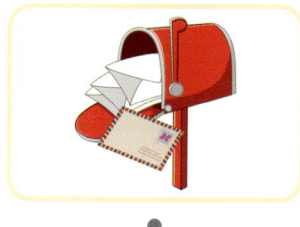

   r d ee

2.

   st t oa

3.

   ai l m

 Change the first letter, write and circle.

1. **joy**
   Change the **j** to **b**.

2. **gray**
   Change the **g** to **p**.

3. **sea**
   Change the **s** to **t**.

Reading Check Up

 A **Read and choose.**

> What is the main idea of this story?

ⓐ We lost all our keys.
ⓑ We found all the seven keys.
ⓒ The boy's mom is sick.

 B **Read and choose the correct answer.**

1. How is the weather now?

rainy

cloudy

sunny

2. What does the lion want?

toast and tea

fruit and juice

bread and jam

3. What blocks the window?

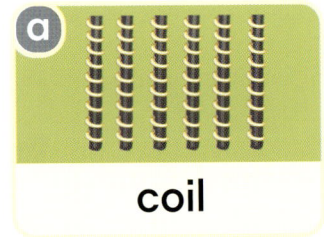
coil

coin

mail

 Read and circle T or F.

1. Kai is a boy but he is brave.　　T　F

2. Kai and Grace lost all their keys.　　T　F

3. The bad lion prays to God.　　T　F

D Look, read and number in order.

This is a great joy.

My mom is very sick.

Please mail a message to our friends.

Chain them up.

Fun Time

Look at the picture and find the word.

Let's Chant!

Track 27

Wow! We found all the seven keys!
The sky is gray. It is going to rain or snow.

My mom is very sick. Let's go and help her.
Good job. Chain them up.

I will push them off to the sea.
I want toast and tea.

Let's pray to God. Oh, Deer!
Please mail a message to our friends.

STORY 10 — The King is Alive!

Track 28-29

 "I can't move my arms."

 "The bad lion will kill us."

 "Bird! Pass a letter to our friends."

 "Shh! A brown cow is looking at us. We can't do anything."

KEYWORDS

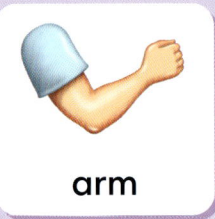				
arm	bird	letter	 brown	cow

 "Everyone, hurry up and climb the top."

 "My foot is hurt. I can't walk fast."

 "Are you having fun?

Clown, have a party.

Push them into the blue sea."

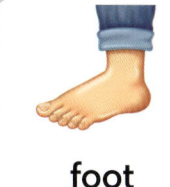
foot

clown

blue

Boom! Boom!

 "Don't worry. We are here."

 "I will save Kai."

 "I will hug Grace like a cloud."

 "Turtle, save the elf."

 "Mouse, go and save the hippo."

 "I will save the short cat."

KEYWORDS

 cloud

 turtle

 mouse

 short

 "Wow! We are here at our house."

 "Open the gold box with the seven keys.

Awake the king with the magic jelly. Call the nurse.

Give the gown and the crown to the king."

 "Good job everyone. Let's have a party.

Cook, bring fruit and juice."

 "Hooray for the king!"

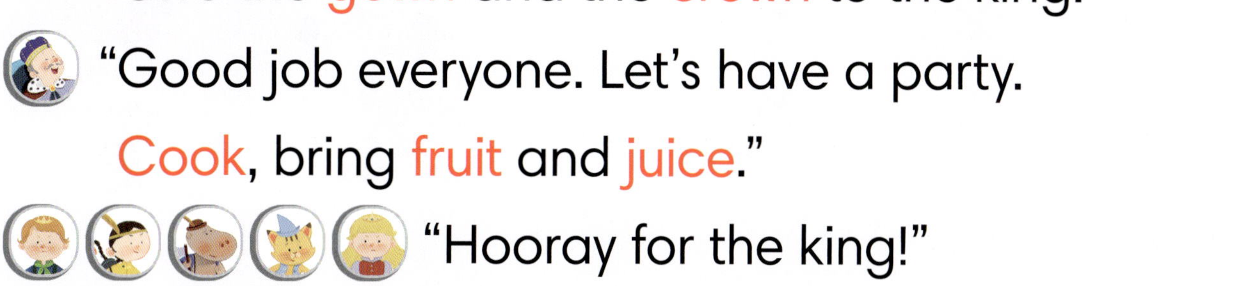

 house

 nurse

 gown

 crown

 cook

 fruit

 juice

Phonics Review

Double Letter Sounds

 A Choose and write the number.

1. ow   2. or   3. ir   4. ur   5. er

B Circle the same double letter vowel sounds.

1.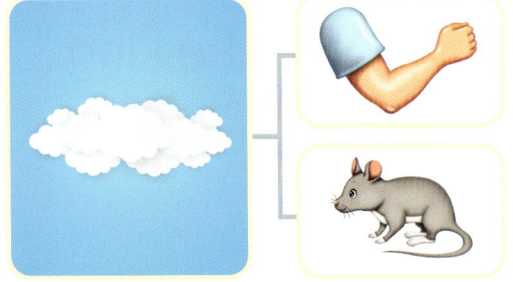

2.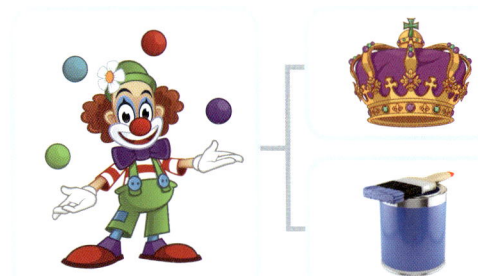

3.

4.

C Circle, complete the word and match.

f o o t c o o k n u r s e s h o r t b i r d a r m

1.

2.

3.

 b_ _d

 c_ _k

sh_ _t

D Circle and complete the sentence.

1.

_____, go and save the hippo.

Mouse / Turtle

2.

_____, have a party.

Clown / Crown

Reading Check Up

 A Read and choose.

> The ending of this story is _____.

ⓐ sad
ⓑ happy
ⓒ not good

 B Look, read and choose.

1.  A _____ cow is looking us.

   ⓐ crown
   ⓑ brown
   ⓒ gown

2.  I can't move my _____.

   ⓐ foot
   ⓑ arms
   ⓒ legs

3.  I will hug Grace like a _____.

   ⓐ mouse
   ⓑ cloud
   ⓒ clown

C **Choose and complete the sentence.**

> letter   crown   foot

1. Bird! Pass a _____ to our friends.

2. My _____ is hurt.

3. Give the gown and the _____ to the king.

D **Look, read and write O or X.**

1. I will save the short cat. ☐

2. Push them into the blue sea. ☐

Fun Time

Match the blocks.

Let's Chant!

Bird! Pass a letter to our friends.
Shh! A brown cow is looking at us.

Clown, have a party.
Push them into the blue sea.

Boom! Boom! Don't worry, we are here.
I will hug Grace like a cloud.
I will save the short cat.

Wow! We are here at our house.
Give the gown and the crown to the king.
Cook and bring fruit and juice.

Glossary

STORY 1

king	apple	bad	dad	gold	box	magic	jelly

key	lion	Indian	elf	cat	elephant	hippo	big

ax	frog	lamp	dog	bread	jam		

STORY 2

white	owl	sky	question	top	wing	yak	net

time	red	tent	zebra	ox	panda	up	

STORY 3

map	dam	ham	six	egg	bag	red	wig

net	dad	mad	man	sad	bad	fish	fin

bed	cat	hit	leg	best			

STORY 4

hot	fog	nut	bun	top	fox	cub	run

lock	hut	rock	jump	rug	up	gum

STORY 5

cave	hate	kite	wave	like	wait	gate	take

mice	game	nine	line	tire	fire	dive	

STORY 6

row	boat	blue	dune	huge	use	rope	mule

fuse	hope	home	bone	move	dome	glue	fruit

juice	cube						

STORY 7

plate	fruit	bread	smell	blade	sled	green	flag

smoke	break	close	crab	clap	blow	trumpet	drum

dress	brush	bride					

STORY 8

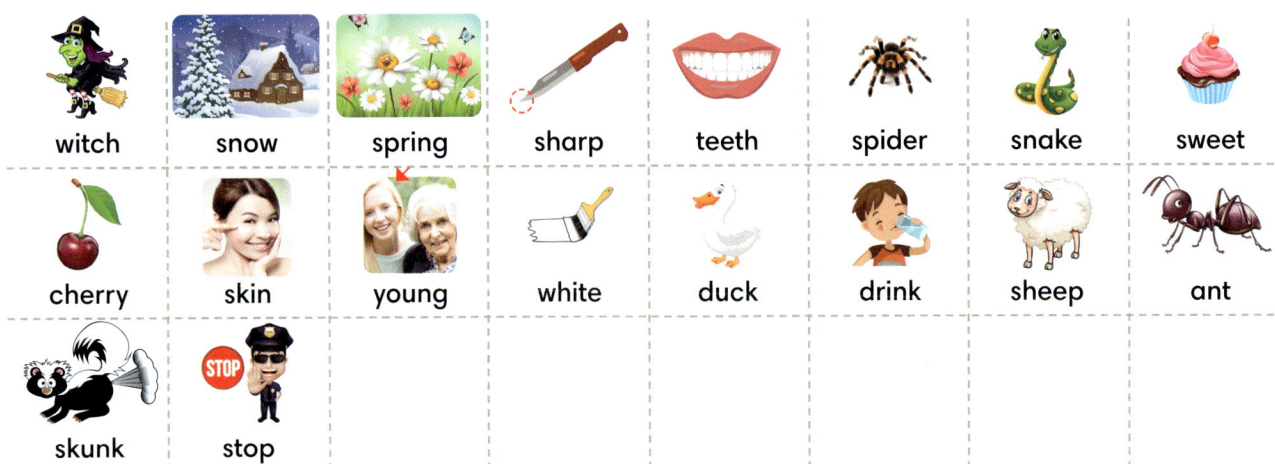

STORY 9

STORY 10